I0142587

The Lighthouses of British Columbia by Harold Stiver

Copyright Statement

Lighthouses of British Columbia
A Guide for Photographers and Explorers

Published by Harold Stiver
Copyright 2025 Harold Stiver

License Notes
All rights reserved. No part of this book may be reproduced in any form or by any electronic or mechanical means including information storage and retrieval systems without permission in writing from the author, except by the reviewer who may quote brief passages
Version 1.0
ISBN 978-1-927835-59-3

Table of Contents

A Short History of Lighthouses

There is some evidence of a lighthouse from the 5th century B.C. of Themistocles of Athens constructing a stone column with a fire on top. This was at the harbour of Piraeus, associated with Athens.

However one of most famous and spectacular early structures was the Lighthouse of Alexandria, or the Pharos of Alexandria. It was one of the Seven Wonders of the Ancient World.

The lighthouse was built in the Third Century B.C. in Alexandria, Egypt by Ptolemy II. It stood on the island of Pharos in the harbour of Alexandria and was said to be 110 metres (350 feet) high.

The lighthouse was built in three stages, a large square at the bottom, an octagonal layer in the middle, and a cylindrical tower at the top.

The structure lasted until a series of earthquakes damaged it, with the 1303 Crete earthquake resulting in its destruction.

The Tower of Hercules, in northwest Spain, is modelled after the Pharos Lighthouse.

The first lighthouse in Canada was built in 1734 in Louisbourg on Cape Breton Island, Nova Scotia. Over the years, the structure was damaged beyond repair in a battle between the British and the French in 1758, destroyed by fire in 1923 and had to be rebuilt several times. The lighthouse known today was built in 1923.

Currently Canada's oldest surviving lighthouse is Sambro Island Lighthouse, built in 1758 at the entrance to Halifax Harbour. It is seen in the image above.

The oldest surviving lighthouse in British Columbia is the Fisgard Lighthouse which opened in 1860. It's the oldest and first pre-Confederation lighthouse in British Columbia and on the west coast. It is located on Fisgard Island at the western entrance to Esquimalt Harbour. It was constructed by John J. Cochrane and John Wright based on plans by architect Joseph Pemberton. It was listed as National Historic Site in 2003.

British Columbia Map

YUKON

NORTH

ALASKA

Prince Rupert

ALBERTA

Queen Charlotte Islands

PACIFIC OCEAN

Vancouver Island

Port Alberni

Vancouver

Nanaimo

Victoria

0   100   200km

SCALE

WASHINGTON

Active Pass (Georgina Point) Lighthouse

The original Active Pass Lighthouse opened in 1985 to aid mariners travelling between Mayne Island and Galiano Island which shortens the journey between Southern Vancouver Island and the Fraser River by several kilometres. This passage became very busy due to the Fraser Gold rush in 1958. This station included a square tower with attached dwelling. The lighthouse was recognized as a Heritage Lighthouse in 2014

Description: White, cylindrical tower

Location: Miners Bay

Directions: From Lighthouse Point, head north on Georgina Point Rd for 350 meters to find the site.

Coordinates: 48°52'24.2"N 123°17'29.4"W

Opened: 1885

Automated: 1997

Deactivated: Active

Height: 10.5 meters, 35 feet

Focal Height: 17.5 meters, 57 feet

Signal: White flash every 10 seconds

Foghorn: Fog alarm building added in 1892

Visitor Access: Grounds open, tower closed

Addenbroke Island Lighthouse

The original Addenbroke Island Lighthouse was erected in 1914 to guide ships travelling the Inside Passage north from the end of Vancouver Island into Fitzhugh Sound. The station also included an oil storage building, a boathouse and a fog bell. It was built by the Department of Marine. The lighting equipment included a 4th order lens. In 1928 the Keeper Ernest Maynard was found murdered. Manuel Hannah was the suspected culprit who had a sketchy past but he disappeared and was not seen again. The current round white tower was opened in 1998.

Description: Fiberglass tower

Location: Port Hardy

Directions: Accessible by boat

Coordinates: 51°36'11.9"N 127°51'49.1"W

Opened: Original 1914, Current 1988

Automated: Still staffed

Deactivated: Active

Height: 8 meters, 26 feet

Focal Height: 24 meters, 79 feet

Signal: White flash every 5 seconds

Foghorn Signal: Fog Bell included at station

Visitor Access: Grounds open, tower closed

Amphitrite Point Lighthouse

The ship The Pass of Melfort was lost with all hands off Amphitrite Point in 1905 in a fierce storm and it produced call for a lighthouse in that area. The original Amphitrite Point Lighthouse opened in 1906 but was destroyed by a tidal wave in 1914. The current tower opened in 1915 to replace it. The tower was not a suitable dwelling and in 1929 a proper keepers dwelling was built. The station was automated in 1916 and continues to be active.

Description: White rectangular tower

Location: Uclewlit

Directions: From Uclewlit, head southeast on Peninsula Rd for 1.2 km and turn right onto Coast Guard Dr where the site is 750 meters.

Coordinates: 48°55'16.3"N125°32'28.1"W

Opened: Original 1906, Current 1915

Automated: 1987

Deactivated: Active

Height: 6 meters, 20 feet

Focal Height: 15 meters, 50 feet

Signal: White flash every 12 seconds

Foghorn Signal: Blast every 20 seconds

Visitor Access: Grounds open, tower closed

Ballenas Island Lighthouse

A lighthouse was proposed for Ballenas Island in 1898 to aid ships travelling the Inside Passage. The original Ballenas Island Lighthouse opened in 1900. William Brown was the first keeper but he was later committed to a lunatic asylum as insane. A fog alarm building was added to the island in 1908 and the lighthouse was moved nearby in 1912 as it was felt to be a superior location. The lighthouse was replaced in 1917 with an octagonal concrete tower. It was automated in 1996 and is still active.

Description: Octagonal concrete tower

Location: Parksville

Directions: Accessible by boat

Coordinates: 49°21'02.0"N 124°09'36.8"W

Opened: Original 1900, Current 1917

Automated: 1996

Deactivated: Active

Height: 11 meters, 35 feet

Focal Height: 21 meters, 70 feet

Signal: White flash every 10 seconds

Foghorn signal: Foghorn added in 1901

Visitor Access: Grounds open, tower closed

Boat Bluff Lighthouse

The original Boat Bluff Light Station opened in 1907 to guide ships travelling to the southern entrance of Tolmie Channel. The station also included 2 keepers dwellings and a fog alarm building The current light is a skeleton tower. The station continues to be staffed and active.

Description: Skeleton tower

Location: Bella Bella

Directions: Accessible by boat

Coordinates: 52°38'34.4"N 128°31'23.2"W

Opened: Original 1907, Current not known

Automated: Still staffed

Deactivated: Active

Height: 7 meters, 24 feet

Focal Height: 11.5 meters, 38 feet

Signal: White/red sector every 5 seconds

Foghorn Signal: Blast every 20 seconds

Visitor Access: Grounds open, tower closed

Brockton Point Lighthouse

Vancouver was growing rapidly after the transcontinental railroad was completed. The original Brockton Point Lighthouse was established in 1890, consisting of lanterns on a mast. It was built to guide ships travelling to and from Vancouver Harbour. The current tower opened in 1915 and was deactivated in 2008.

Description: White, square pyramidal tower

Location: Vancouver

Directions: 2157 Stanley Park Dr, Vancouver

Coordinates: 49.300917°N 123.117018°W

Opened: Original 1890, Current 1915

Automated: 1956

Deactivated: 2008

Height: 10,5 meters, 35 feet

Focal Height: 12.5 meters, 41 feet

Signal: Fixed white with red sector

Foghorn : Fog bell

Visitor Access: Grounds open, tower closed

Cape Beale Lighthouse

The original Cape Beale Lighthouse opened in 1874 and was the first lighthouse to be erected on the western coast of Vancouver Island. The work was directed by Charles Hayward for this light which marks the southern entrance to Barkley Sound. The tower was in poor condition and was replaced by the present tower in 1958. It continues to be staffed and active.

Description: Red skeleton tower

Location: Bamfield

Directions: The site may be reached from a 7.5 km. trail originating just south of Bamfield. It is strenuous and portions may be under water outside of low tide.

Coordinates: 48°47'11.3"N 125°12'55.8"W

Opened: Original 1874, Current 1958

Automated: Still staffed

Deactivated: Active

Height: 10 meters, 33 feet

Focal Height: 51 meters, 167 feet

Signal: Fixed red/white sector

Foghorn: 2 Airchime fog horns

Visitor Access: Grounds open, tower occasionally accompanied by keeper.

Cape Mudge (Quadra Island) Lighthouse

The original Cape Mudge or Quadra Island Lighthouse opened in 1898 to guide ships to the southern entrance to Discovery Passage which is a few miles south of the treacherous Seymour Narrows and the dangerous submerged Ripple Rock. G.H. Frost fulfilled the contact for its construction. Ripple Rock would claim over 100 more vessels before it was tunnelled and destroyed by explosives. The lighting equipment was upgraded with a 5th order Fresnel lens in 1908. The current tower replaced the original in 1916. It continues to be staffed and active.

Description: White octagonal tower

Location: Campbell River

Directions: From Campbell River, take the ferry to Quathiaski Cove on Quadra Island. Head south on Green Rd for 1.1 km and turn left onto Noble Rd. After 1.0 km turn right onto Cape Mudge Rd and in 3.0 km turn right onto Joyce Rd where the site is 1 km.

Coordinates: 49°59'54.8"N125°11'43.9"W

Opened: Original 1898, Current 1916

Automated: Still staffed

Deactivated: Active

Height: 12 meters, 40 feet

Focal Height: 17.5 meters, 58 feet

Signal: Fixed red/white sector

Foghorn: Fog signal building added in 1913

Visitor Access: Grounds open, tower open spring and summer

Cape Scott Lighthouse

The original Cape Scott Light was a lantern on a mast installed in 1927 at the western tip of Vancouver Island. A radar station was opened nearby during World War II to guard against enemy aircraft. A skeleton tower replaced the original in 1981. It continues to be staffed and active.

Description: Square skeleton tower

Location: Holberg

Directions: From the Cape Scott Provincial Park parking lot, take Cape Scott Trail leads 23.6 km (14.8 miles) north to Cape Scott Lighthouse

Coordinates: 50°46'57.0"N 128°25'38.0"W

Opened: Original 1927, Current 1981

Automated: Still staffed

Deactivated: Active

Height: 9 meters, 29 feet

Focal Height: 70 meters, 229 feet

Signal: White flash every 10 seconds

Foghorn: Fog alarm building added 1959

Visitor Access: Grounds open, tower closed

Carmanah Point Lighthouse

A lighthouse was approved for Point Bonilla in 1890 as an aid to ships travelling the Strait of Juan de Fuca The contract was awarded to George H. Frost. The building materials were unloaded in a dense fog and it was later found to be Carmanah Point rather then Point Bonilla. It was decided to locate the station there rather than move all the supplies. The original site opened in 1891. The current tower replaced it in 1920. The light continues to be active. It was automated in 2024.

Description: White octagonal tower

Location: Port Renfrew

Directions: The site is on the West Coast Trail in the Pacific Rim National Park Reserve about 20 km (13 mi) northwest of the Gordon River Trailhead near Port Renfrew.

Coordinates: 48°36'42.1"N 124°45'04.7"W

Opened: Original 1891, Current 1920

Automated: 2024

Deactivated: Active

Height: 11 meters, 36 feet

Focal Height: 66.5 meters, 182 feet

Signal: White flash every 5 seconds

Foghorn Signal: N/A

Visitor Access: Grounds open, tower closed

Chatham Point Lighthouse

The original Chatham Point Lighthouse was opened in 1908 to designate the point where the Discovery Passage makes an abrupt turn to Johnstone Strait. In 1957 the current tower was built to replace the original as well as a fog control building, a boathouse and new keeper's dwellings. The station continues to be staffed and active.

Description: White cylindrical tower

Location: Campbell River

Directions: Accessible by boat

Coordinates: 50°20'00.2"N 125°26'25.8"W

Opened: Original 1908, Current 1957

Automated: Still staffed

Deactivated: Active

Height: 4.5 meters, 15 feet

Focal Height: 6.5 meters, 21 feet

Signal: Green flash every 5 seconds

Foghorn signal: Blast every 20 seconds

Visitor Access: Closed

Chrome Island Lighthouse

The original Chrome Island Lighthouse opened in 1891 as a guide to ships travelling the southern entrance to Baynes Sound. The contract for a tower attached to a keeper's dwelling was fulfilled by J. A. Brittancourt. Two range lights were built in 1898 and the original tower was removed from the dwelling. In 1989 a skeleton tower was erected. The station is still staffed and continues to be active.

Description: Cylindrical tower

Location: Denman Island

Directions: Accessible by boat

Coordinates: 49°28'19.9"N 124°41'02.0"W

Opened: Original 1891, Second 1898, Current 1989

Automated: Still staffed

Deactivated: Active

Height: 7.5 meters, 25 feet

Focal Height: 22 meters, 72 feet

Signal: Fixed yellow

Foghorn : Diaphone foghorn in 1908

Visitor Access: Grounds open, tower closed

Discovery Island Lighthouse

The original Discovery Island Lighthouse was opened in 1886 after being built by Alex Mennie as a guide to the southwest side of the entrance to Haro Strait. The first keeper was Richard Brinn who passed away in 1901. His daughter Mary Croft was appointed, becoming Canada's first female lightkeeper. The current tower was erected in 1970. The light was automated in 1997 and continues to be active.

Description: White cylindrical tower

Location: Victoria

Directions: Accessible by boat

Coordinates: 48°25'28.6"N 123°13'32.4"W

Opened: Original 1886, Second 1958, Current 1970

Automated: 1997

Deactivated: Active

Height: 11.5 meters, 38 feet

Focal Height: 28 meters, 92 feet

Signal: White flash every 5 seconds

Foghorn signal: Blast every 68 seconds

Visitor Access: Grounds open, tower closed

Dryad Point Lighthouse

The original Dryad Point Lighthouse was erected in 1899 to mark the Lama Passage and Seaforth Channel. The lighting was a 7th order lens. A hand foghorn was added to the site in 1901. The current lighthouse replaced the original in 1919. There were plans to automate the station but they were changed and the station remains staffed and active.

Description: White square tower

Location: Bella Bella

Directions: Accessible by boat

Coordinates: 52°11'06.5"N 128°06'42.0"W

Opened: Original 1899, Current 1919

Automated: Still staffed

Deactivated: Active

Height: 8.5 meters, 28 feet

Focal Height: 11.5 meters, 38 feet

Signal: White/red sector every 5 seconds

Foghorn: Hand foghorn added in 1901

Visitor Access: Grounds open, tower closed

Entrance Island Lighthouse

The original Entrance Island Lighthouse opened in 1876 to guide ships travelling Georgia Strait. The initial two contractors for this contract failed to finish it and it was finally completed by Arthur Finney. The third Keeper was M.G. Clark who was known to hire assistants and have them do the work at the station as well as his nearby ranch. The station continues to be staffed and active.

Description: White cylindrical tower

Location: Gabriola

Directions: Accessible by boat

Coordinates: 49°12'33.2"N 123°48'29.2"W

Opened: Original 1876, Current 1970

Automated: Still staffed

Deactivated: Active

Height: 14 meters, 45 feet

Focal Height: 19 meters, 62 feet

Signal: White flash every 5 seconds

Foghorn: Foghorn added in 1894

Visitor Access: Closed

Estevan Point Lighthouse

The Estevan Point Lighthouse, with its flying buttresses, is one of the most beautiful in Canada. Due to heavy shipping off Vancouver Island's West Coast, the Canadian Government budgeted for a light at Estevan Point in 1907 and it opened in 1910. It included the tower, keeper's dwellings and a fog control building. The light was unlit for a period in 1918 after being damaged by an earthquake. The site continues to be staffed and active.

Description: Octagonal concrete tower with flying buttresses

Location: Gold River

Directions: Accessible by boat

Coordinates: 49°22'59.0"N 126°32'39.0"W

Opened: 1910

Automated: Still staffed

Deactivated: Active

Height: 30.5 meters, 100 feet

Focal Height: 37.5 meters, 123 feet

Signal: 2 white flash every 15 seconds

Foghorn Signal: Fog alarm building added in 1908

Visitor Access: Grounds open, tower closed

Fisgard Lighthouse

The Fisgard Lighthouse opened in 1860 as protection for ships entering Esquimalt Harbour and became the first lighthouse in British Columbia. The work was contracted by John Wright. The lighting equipment was a 4th order Fresnel lens. In 2010 a major restoration was completed in time for its 150th anniversary. The station was listed as a National Historic Place in 1958.

Description: White cylindrical tower

Location: Victoria

Directions: 603 Fort Rodd Hill Rd, Victoria

Coordinates: 48°25'49.4"N123°26'51.4"W

Opened: 1860

Automated: 1929

Deactivated: Active

Height: 14.5 meters, 48 feet

Focal Height: 21.5 meters, 71 feet

Signal: White/red flash every 4 seconds

Foghorn Signal: N/A

Visitor Access: Grounds and tower open

Green Island Lighthouse

The original Green Island Lighthouse opened in 1905 as an aid to ships travelling to Skagway and other northern destinations. A need for this light was prompted by the wreck of the Bristol in 1902 which ran aground on Green island in 1902 with the loss of 7 lives. The lighting equipment was a 3rd order Fresnel lens. A hand foghorn was added to the station in 1919 and updated to a diaphone alarm in 1949. The site is still staffed and active.

Description: White octagonal tower

Location: Prince Rupert

Directions: Accessible by boat

Coordinates: 54°34'07.0"N 130°42'31.5"W

Opened: Original 1906, Current 1957

Automated: Still staffed

Deactivated: Active

Height: 10.5 meters, 35 feet

Focal Height: 19 meters, 63 feet

Signal: White flash every 5 seconds

Foghorn: Hand foghorn added 1919

Visitor Access: Grounds open, tower closed

Ivory Island Lighthouse

The original Ivory Island Lighthouse was opened in 1898 to protect ships travelling north where the route is unprotected from the Pacific Ocean. The station was subject to heavy gales and the boathouse was destroyed in the first year. In 1908 a tidal wave destroyed the newly erected fog control building. It was replaced by a steel tower in 1957 but this was also lost to a 1982 storm. The current tower opened in 1983 and the station remains staffed and active.

Description: Red skeleton tower

Location: Bella Bella

Directions: Accessible by boat

Coordinates: 52°16'11.2"N 128°24'24.8"W

Opened: Original 1898, Second 1957, Current 1983

Automated: Still staffed

Deactivated: Active

Height: 5 meters, 17 feet

Focal Height: 20.5 meters, 67 feet

Signal: White flash every 5 seconds

Foghorn Signal: Blast every 60 seconds

Visitor Access: Grounds open, tower closed

Langara Lighthouse

The building of the Grand Trunk Pacific Railway with its terminal at Prince Rupert generated a need for a lighthouse at the north end of Haida Gwaii (formerly Queen Charlotte Islands) to mark the Dixon Entrance approach. In 1913 the Langara Lighthouse opened. It was equipped with 1st order Fresnel lens which is the only one still in use in Canada as the site is active and staffed.

Description: White octagonal tower

Location: Masset

Directions: Accessible by boat

Coordinates: 54°15'19.4"N 133°03'33.8"W

Opened: 1913

Automated: Still staffed

Deactivated: Active

Height: 7.5 meters, 25 feet

Focal Height: 59 meters, 160 feet

Signal: White flash every 5 seconds

Foghorn: Fog alarm plant

Visitor Access: Grounds open, tower closed

Lennard Island Lighthouse

The original Lennard Island Lighthouse was opened in 1904 to aid mariners travelling Clayoquot Sound and those travelling from Asia. A fog alarm building was added 1905. A fire destroyed the keepers dwelling in 1927 and was replaced the next year. In 1968 a new fibreglass tower was prefabricated in Tofino and transported to the site by helicopter. The light continues to be active.

Description: White cylindrical tower

Location: Tifino

Directions: Accessible by boat

Coordinates: 49°06'37.5"N 125°55'24.7"W

Opened: Original 1904, Current 1968

Automated: Still staffed

Deactivated: Active

Height: 18 meters, 58 feet

Focal Height: 35 meters, 115 feet

Signal: White flash every 10 seconds

Foghorn: Fog alarm building added 1905

Visitor Access: Grounds open, tower closed

Lucy Islands Lighthouse

In 1907 the Lucy Islands Lighthouse was opened to guide ships travelling to Prince Rupert and the Transcanada Railway terminal. The current tower replaced it in 1960 along with a new dwelling. The station was automated in 1988 and is still active.

Description: Octagonal concrete tower

Location: Prince Rupert

Directions: Accessible by boat

Coordinates: 54°17'44.6"N 130°36'31.6"W

Opened: Original 1907, Current 1960

Automated: 1988

Deactivated: Active

Height: 10.5 meters, 35 feet

Focal Height: 31.5 meters, 71 feet

Signal: Red flash every 6 seconds

Foghorn signal: N/A

Visitor Access: Closed

Merry Island Lighthouse

Ships travelling north from Vancouver may enter Welcome Passage between Thormanby Island and the mainland and Merry Island is at the south entrance. The original Merry Island Lighthouse was opened in 1903 to aid these vessels. The fog signal equipment was upgraded in 1924. In 1966 the current tower replaced the original and electrical and telephone cables were installed. The site continues to be staffed and active.

Description: White square tower

Location: Halfmoon Bay

Directions: Accessible by boat

Coordinates: 49°28'02.8"N 123°54'44.3"W

Opened: Original 1902, Current 1966

Automated: Still staffed

Deactivated: Active

Height: 12 meters, 40 feet

Focal Height: 18 meters, 60 feet

Signal: White flash every 15 seconds

Foghorn: Hand foghorn added 1903

Visitor Access: Closed

Nootka Lighthouse

A 1906 petition requesting a lighthouse to mark the entrance to Nootka Sound was answered when the original Nootka Lighthouse was erected on San Rafael Island. The hand foghorn was updated with a diaphone fog alarm in 1927. The station continues to be staffed and active.

Description: Square pyramidal steel skeletal tower with square central cylinder

Location: San Rafael Island

Directions: Accessible by boat

Coordinates: 49°35'33.5"N 126°36'55.4"W

Opened: Original 1911, Current 1958

Automated: Still staffed

Deactivated: Active

Height: 6 meters, 19 feet

Focal Height: 31 meters, 101 feet

Signal: White flash every 12 seconds

Foghorn: Diaphone fog alarm added in 1927

Visitor Access: Grounds open, tower closed

Ogden Point Breakwater Lighthouse

In 1916 the 244 meter (600 feet) Ogden Point Breakwater was built and the following year the Ogden Point Breakwater Lighthouse was erected at its tip. Parfitt Brothers completed the work on the lighthouse which guides ships into Victoria Harbour. A fog alarm was added in 1919 and an electricity cable in 1926. The light continues to be active.

Description: White tower, red band at bottom

Location: Victoria

Directions: From Dallas Road and Dock St. intersection in Victoria, you can access the breakwater with the lighthouse at the tip

Coordinates: 48°24'48.6"N 123°23'37.8"W

Opened: 1917

Automated: 1917

Deactivated: Active

Height: 7 meters, 23 feet

Focal Height: 12 meters, 39 feet

Signal: Red flash every second

Foghorn: Electrically operated fog alarm added in 1919

Visitor Access: Grounds open, tower closed

Pachena Point Lighthouse

A lighthouse for Pachena Point had been proposed for some years but it was the wreck of the Valencia which ran aground there in 1906 that prompted it proceeding. 133 people died and no women or children survived. The Pachena Point Lighthouse opened in 1908. A lifesaving system was also developed in this dense forest area which involved building a road, bridges and supplies for survivors . The station was restored in 2016 and is still active.

Description: White, octagonal tower

Location: Bamfield

Directions: The West Coast Trail can be accessed just east of Bamfield and it is 20 km (12.5 miles) for a return trip to the lighthouse.

Coordinates: 48°43'19.6"N125°05'51.2"W

Opened: 1908

Automated: 2024

Deactivated: Active

Height: 20 meters, 66 feet

Focal Height: 47 meters, 154 feet

Signal: 2 white flashes every 7.5 seconds

Foghorn: Fog alarm building added 1908

Visitor Access: Grounds open, tower closed

Pilot Bay Lighthouse

The Pilot Bay Lighthouse opened in 1904 on Pilot Peninsula to guide passenger sternwheelers on Kootenay Lake. In 1920 the signal was changed from fixed white to a white flash every 12 seconds. The lighthouse was repaired by Tugawar Enterprises Ltd in 1985. In 2003, the Traditional Timber Framing Company added two windows to the south side, as it originally had. The light was deactivated in 1993.

Description: Square pyramidal frame tower

Location: Kootenay Bay

Directions: From Kootenay Bay, head southeast on Pilot Bay Rd for 4.2 km to find the site

Coordinates: 49°38'19.8"N 116°53'04.4"W

Opened: 1904

Automated: 1920

Deactivated: 1993

Height: 7.5 meters, 25 feet

Focal Height: 11 meters, 37 feet

Signal: White flash every 12 seconds

Foghorn signal: N/A

Visitor Access: Grounds and tower open

Pine Island Lighthouse

The original Pine Island Lighthouse opened in 1907 to aid mariners travelling Queen Charlotte Sound. The station includes a dwelling and fog-alarm building. In 1967 a storm with gale force winds hit the site and a 50 foot wave hit the station which destroyed the fog signal building, the fuel tanks and a radio beacon. The current lighthouse, a cylindrical white tower, was opened in 2001 and remains active.

Description: Cylindrical white tower

Location: Prince Rupert

Directions: Accessible by boat

Coordinates: 50°58'32.2"N 127°43'40.7"W

Opened: Original 1907, Current 2001

Automated: Still staffed

Deactivated: Active

Height: 10.5 meters, 35 feet

Focal Height: 28 meters, 93 feet

Signal: Red flash every 10 seconds

Foghorn Signal: Blast every 2 minutes

Visitor Access: Grounds open, tower closed

Point Atkinson Lighthouse

The original Point Atkinson Lighthouse opened as the first lighthouse in the Vancouver area and guided ships into Vancouver Harbour. The contract was fulfilled by Arthur Finney. The tower arose from the attached dwelling. A foghorn was added in 1889 and updated to a diaphone fog alarm in 1902. The current lighthouse was erected in 1912 and continues to be active.

Description: White hexagonal tower

Location: West Vancouver

Directions: From the north end of Lion's Gate Bridge, take Marine Drive west for 11.1 km (6.9 miles), and then turn left onto Beacon Lane where there is a parking area available.

Coordinates: 49°19'49.0"N 123°15'53.0"W

Opened: Original 1875, Current 1912

Automated: 1996

Deactivated: Active

Height: 18 meters, 60 feet

Focal Height: 33 meters, 108 feet

Signal: 2 white flashes every 5 seconds

Foghorn: Hand foghorn added in 1889

Visitor Access: Grounds open, tower closed

Porlier Pass Rear Range Light

In 1901, petitions were made to the Department of Marine for range lights to guide ships through the Porlier Pass. The range lights opened in 1902 with the front range on Race Point and the rear range on Virago Point. A keeper's dwelling was added in 1907.

Description: White square tower

Location: Sturdies Bay

Directions: From the ferry landing at Sturdies Bay, head northwest on Sturdies Bay Rd for 2.7 km and turn right onto Porlier Pass Rd. After 1.7 km, turn left to stay on Porlier Pass Rd and the site is 21.3 km. The last 1 km. is Penelakut tribal land and permission to walk the trail is needed.

Coordinates: 49°00'46.4"N 123°35'09.2"W

Opened: 1902

Automated: 1996

Deactivated: Active

Height: 7.5 meters, 25 feet

Focal Height: 10 meters, 34 feet

Signal: Fixed yellow

Foghorn: Hand foghorn

Visitor Access: Grounds open, tower closed

Port Alberni Lighthouse

The Port Alberni Lighthouse is known as Port Alberni's Maritime Discovery Centre. The dwelling houses an exhibit of local maritime history. The lantern was originally at the Chrome Island Lighthouse and was donated to the museum. The lighthouse was renovated in 2022.

Description: Square pyramidal wood tower

Location: Port Alberni

Directions: 2750 Harbour Road, Port Alberni

Coordinates: 49°13'52.9"N 124°48'49.6"W

Opened: 2001

Automated: 2001

Deactivated: Active

Height: 11 meters, 36 feet

Focal Height: 13 meters, 43 feet

Signal: White flash every 123 seconds

Foghorn signal: N/A

Visitor Access: Grounds open, museum open during summer

Portlock Point Lighthouse

The original Portlock Point Lighthouse was opened in 1895 to guide vessels travelling between Swanson and Trincomali Channels between Vancouver and Victoria. The contract was fulfilled by G. Frost. A fog bell was added the next year. In 1964 a kerosene explosion killed the keeper and destroyed the dwelling. At that point the station was automated and continues to be active.

Description: White tower with red top

Location: Prevost Island

Directions: Accessible by boat

Coordinates: 48°49'40.4"N 123°21'06.8"W

Opened: Original 1895, Current 1987

Automated: 1964

Deactivated: Active

Height: 7.5 meters, 25 feet

Focal Height: 15.5 meters, 51 feet

Signal: Flashing white

Foghorn: Hand foghorn

Visitor Access: Closed

Prospect Point Lighthouse

The original Prospect Point Lighthouse opened in 1898 just after the opening of Stanley Park. It was built to guide ships travelling to Vancouver Harbour. The current structure opened in 1948. It is made of reinforced concrete and was built by J.C. Dill.

Description: White tower, red band at top

Location: Stanley Park, Vancouver

Directions: The point on the south side of Vancouver Harbour a short distance west of the Lion's Gate Bridge

Coordinates: 49°18'50.7"N 123°08'29.3"W

Opened: Original 1898, Current 1948

Automated: 1926

Deactivated: Active

Height: 11.5 meters, 38 feet

Focal Height: 13 meters, 42 feet

Signal: Red flash every 2 seconds

Foghorn: Fog bell

Visitor Access: Grounds open, tower closed

Pulteney Point Lighthouse

The original Pulteney Point Lighthouse was built to mark the detachment of the Broughton and Queen Charlotte Straits. The current square concrete tower replaced the original in 1943 with a fog signal building erected as well.

Description: White square tower

Location: Sointula

Directions: From Sointula, head north on 1 St toward Bere Rd form 300 meters and turn right onto Bere Rd. After 650 meters, turn left onto Pulteney Point Rd and drive 11.2 km to the site.

Coordinates: 50°37'49.9"N 127°09'18.9"W

Opened: Original 1905, Current 1943

Automated: Still staffed

Deactivated: Active

Height: 9 meters, 30 feet

Focal Height: 12 meters, 40 feet

Signal: Red flash every 10 seconds

Foghorn Signal: 3 blasts every 60 seconds

Visitor Access: Grounds open, tower closed

Race Rocks Lighthouse

The Race Rocks Lighthouse opened in 1861 to aid ships passing a group of rocks at the southeast of Vancouver Island. It is the second oldest lighthouse on the west coast of Canada. Stone used to build the station was quarried on the island. A fog bell was added in 1867 and this was updated to a steam powered alarm in 1875. The lighthouse was restored in 2009.

Description: Cylindrical tower, black and and white bands

Location: Metchosin

Directions: Accessible by boat

Coordinates: 48°17'52.9"N123°31'53.1"W

Opened: 1861

Automated: 1997

Deactivated: Active

Height: 24.5 meters, 80 feet

Focal Height: 36 meters, 118 feet

Signal: White flash every 10 seconds

Foghorn Signal: 3 blasts every 60 seconds

Visitor Access: Closed

Scarlett Point Lighthouse

The original Scarlett Point Lighthouse opened in 1905 to aid ships travelling to the entrance of Christie Passage. The original tower was replaced by a skeleton tower in 1965. The station continues to be staffed and is still active.

Description: White cylindrical tower

Location: Port Hardy

Directions: Accessible by boat

Coordinates: 50°51'37.9"N 127°36'45.1"W

Opened: Original 1905, Current 1965

Automated: Still staffed

Deactivated: Active

Height: 11 meters, 37 feet

Focal Height: 24 meters, 78 feet

Signal: White flash every 5 seconds

Foghorn: Foghorn added in 1907

Visitor Access: Grounds open, tower closed

Sheringham Point Lighthouse

The Sheringham Point Lighthouse was erected in 1912 as an aid to ships travelling the Strait of Juan de Fuca. The station was built by Thomas Stedham. The site included the tower, a fog alarm building, a boathouse and a dwelling. The lighthouse was designated a Heritage Place in 2015. It remains active.

Description: White hexagonal tower

Location: Sooke

Directions: From Shirley, head south on Sheringham Point Rd for 1.7 km to find the site

Coordinates: 48°22'36.1"N 123°55'15.6"W

Opened: 1912

Automated: 1989

Deactivated: Active

Height: 19.5 meters, 64 feet

Focal Height: 22 meters, 72 feet

Signal: Green flash every 15 seconds

Foghorn: Fog alarm building

Visitor Access: Closed

Sisters Islets Lighthouse

The original Sisters Islets Lighthouse was built by George H. Frost and opened in 1898 as an aid to ships travelling the Strait of Georgia. The isolated site and poor conditions made it hard to retain keepers and the station had 5 in the first 6 years. A 4th order Fresnel lens updated the lighting equipment in 1914. The site received a new tower in 1967. The light was automated in 1996 and remains active.

Description: White cylindrical tower

Location: Parksville

Directions: Accessible by boat

Coordinates: 49°29'12.3"N 124°26'05.2"W

Opened: Original 1898, Current 1967

Automated: 1996

Deactivated: Active

Height: 18 meters, 60 feet

Focal Height: 21 meters, 70 feet

Signal: 2 white flashes every 15 seconds

Foghorn Signal: 2 blasts every 90 seconds

Visitor Access: Closed

Trial Islands Lighthouse

The original Trial Islands Lighthouse opened in 1906 at Staines Point as a guide to ships using the Enterprise Channel. The original tower was replaced by a cylindrical concrete tower in 1970. In 2009 the Canadian government was looking at destaffing the light but these plans were dropped in 2010. The site remains active.

Description: White cylindrical tower

Location: Victoria

Directions: Accessible by boat

Coordinates: 48°23'42.4"N 123°18'18.7"W

Opened: Original 1906, Current 1970

Automated: Still staffed

Deactivated: Active

Height: 13 meters, 42 feet

Focal Height: 28 meters, 93 feet

Signal: Green flash every 5 seconds

Foghorn Signal: Blast every 60 seconds

Visitor Access: Closed

Triangle Island Lighthouse

The Triangle Island Lighthouse was built to mark the entrance to Queen Charlotte Sound. It was situated at the 680 foot summit of Triangle Island. This turned out to be a poor location as it often experienced very high winds blowing in from the Pacific Ocean. The Department of the Marine recognized the problem and dismantled the station. In 2004 the Sooke Region Historical Society asked the Coast Guard for the Lantern Room and Fresnel lens which they agreed to and it became part of the Sooke Region Museum.

Description: Short white tower

Location: Sooke

Directions: 2070 Phillips Road in Sooke

Coordinates: 48°23'02.9"N 123°42'21.9"W

Opened: 1910

Automated: N/A

Deactivated: 1919

Height: 8 meters, 26 feet

Focal Height: N/A

Signal: N/A

Foghorn signal: N/A

Visitor Access: Grounds open, tower closed

Triple Island Lighthouse

The Triple Island Lighthouse opened in 1920 as an aid to ships using the Brown Passage to reach Prince Rupert. The contract for the work was completed by J.H. Hilditch. The lighting equipment was a 3rd order Fresnel lens and the fog control was a diaphone fog alarm. The station continues to be staffed and active.

Description: White octagonal tower

Location: Prince Rupert

Directions: Accessible by boat

Coordinates: 54°17'41.0"N 130°52'50.0"W

Opened: 1920

Automated: Still staffed

Deactivated: Active

Height: 22 meters, 72 feet

Focal Height: 28 meters, 92 feet

Signal: 2 white flashes every 9 seconds

Foghorn signal: Blast every 30 seconds

Visitor Access: Closed

Other Lighthouses

Name: Bonilla Island   **Location**: Prince Rupert
Opened: 1960   **Access**: Grounds open, tower closed
Coordinates: 53°29'33.1"N 130°38'15.0"W

Name: East Point   **Location**: Saturna Island
Opened: 1888   **Access**: Grounds open, tower closed
Coordinates: 48°46'58.8"N 123°02'43.7"W

Name: Egg Island   **Location**: Port Hardy
Opened: 1964   **Access**: Grounds open, tower closed
Coordinates: 51°14'53.7"N 127°50'01.5"W

Name: McInnes Island   **Location**: Bella Bella
Opened: 1954   **Access**: Grounds open, tower closed
Coordinates: 52°15'41.2"N 128°43'18.4"W

Name: Quatsino   **Location**: Kains Island
Opened: 1977   **Access**: Grounds open, tower closed
Coordinates: 50°26'28.3"N 128°01'56.8"W

Name: Sand Heads   **Location**: Richmond
Opened: 2002   **Access**: Closed
Coordinates: 49°06'21.2"N 123°18'11.9"W

Vancouver Tour

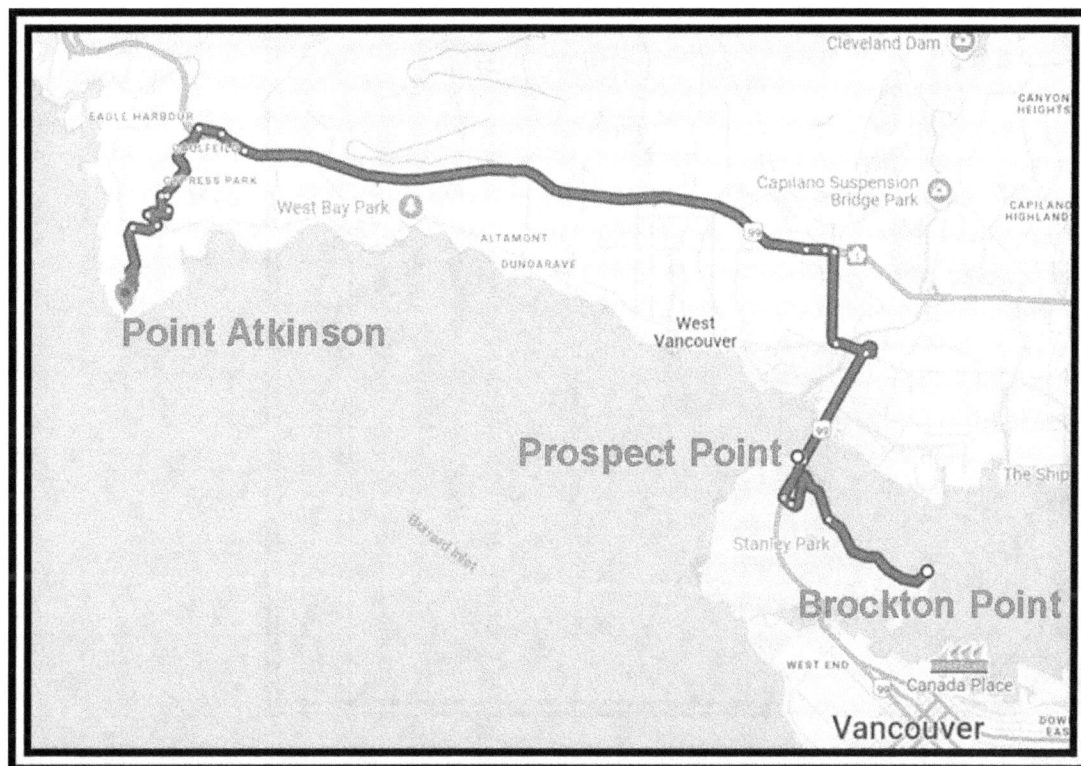

3 lighthouses, 30 minutes driving

Brockton Point	49°18'03.3"N 123°07'01.3"W
Prospect Point	49°18'50.7"N 123°08'29.3"W
Point Atkinson	49°19'49.0"N 123°15'53.0"W

Victoria Tour

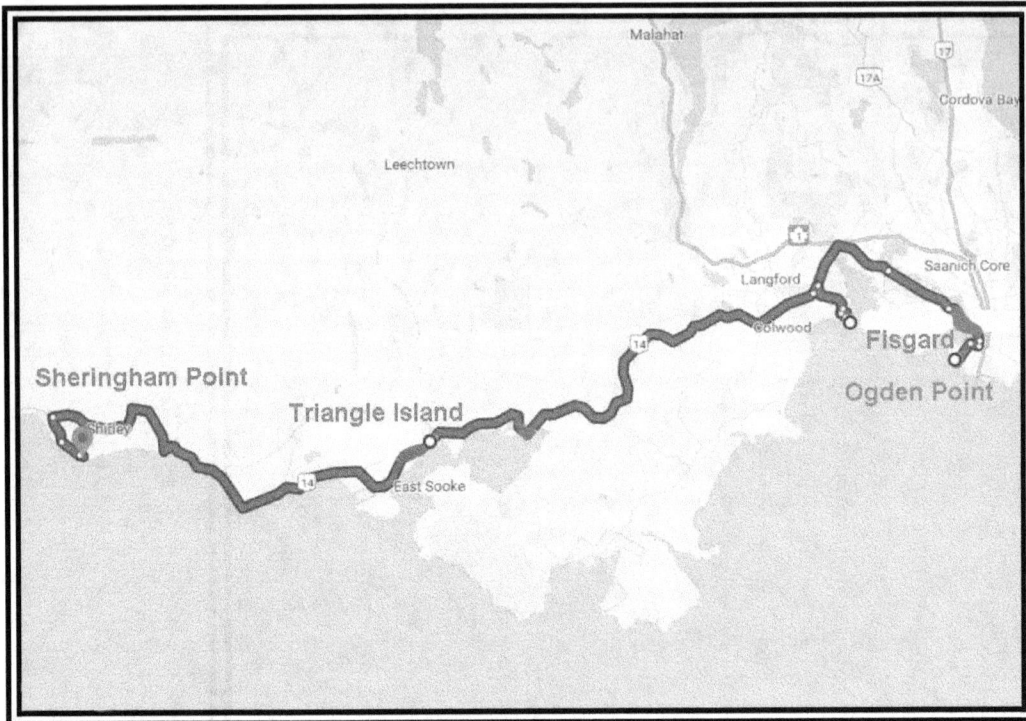

4 lighthouses, 1 hour 30 minutes driving

Ogden Point Breakwater	48°24'54.6"N 123°23'01.7"W
Fisgard	48°25'49.4"N 123°26'51.4"W
Triangle Island	48°23'02.9"N 123°42'21.9"W
Sheringham Point	48°22'36.1"N 123°55'15.6"W

Glossary of Lighthouse Terms

Aerobeacon: A lighting system which creates a signal over long distances. It consists of a strong light source with a focusing mechanism which is rotated on a vertical axis. It has been used at airports as well as lighthouses.

Acetylene: After 1910, acetylene began to be used to power the lighthouse light source. It has the advantage that it could be stored on site with a sun valve turning it on at dusk and off at daybreak.

Alternating Light: A light source which changes colours in a regular pattern.

Arc of Visibility: The range of the horizon from which the lighthouse is visible from the sea.

Automated: A lighthouse that operates without a keeper. The light functions are controlled by timers, and light and fog detectors.

Beacon: A fixed aid to navigation.

Bell: A sound signal produced by fixed aids and by sea movement on buoys.

Breakwater: A structure that protects a shore area or harbour by blocking waves.

Bull's-eye Lens: A convex lens used to refract light.

Catwalk: An elevated walkway which allows the keeper to move in the lantern room in towers built in the sea.

Characteristic: The distinct pattern of the flashing light or foghorn blast which allows seamen to distinguish which light station it is coming from.

Chariot: A wheeled assembly at the bottom of a Fresnel lens which is rotated around a circular track.

Clockwork Mechanism: Early lighthouses had a series of gears, pulleys and weights, which had to be wound on a recurring basis by the keepers.

Cottage Style Lighthouse: A lighthouse made up of a keeper's residence with a light on top.

Crib: A base structure filled with stone which acted as the foundation for the structure built on top.

Daymark: A unique colour pattern that identifies a specific lighthouse during the day.

Decommissioned: A lighthouse that has discontinued operating as a aid to navigation.

Diaphone: A sound signal produced by a slotted piston moved by compressed air.

Directional Light: A light which marks the direction to be followed.

Eclipse: The interval between light flashed or foghorn blasts.

Fixed Light: A light shining continuously without periods of eclipse or darkness.

Flashing Light: Alight pattern distinguished by periods of eclipse or darkness.

Focal Plane: The path of a beam of light emitted from a lighthouse. The height from the center of the beam to the sea is known as the height of the focal plane.

Fog Detector: A device used to automatically determine conditions which may reduce visibility and the need to start a sound signal.

Fog Signal: An audible device such as a bell or horn that warns seamen during period of fog when the light would be ineffective.

Fresnel Lens: An optic system composed of a convex lens and prisms which concentrate the light beam through a series of prisms. The design was produced by Augustin Fresnel in the 1800s.

Geographic Range: The longest distance the curvature of the earth allows an object of a certain height to be seen.

Isophase Light: A light in which the duration of light and darkness are equal.

Keeper: The person responsible for the maintenance and operation of the lighthouse.

Lamp and Reflector: A lamp and polished mirror used before the invention of more effective optic systems such as the Fresnel lens.

Lantern: A glass covered space at the top of the lighthouse tower, which housed the lighting equipment.

Lens: The glass optical system used to concentrate and direct the light.

Light Sector: The arc over which a light can be seen from the sea.

Lightship: A ship that served as a lighthouse.

Light Station: The lighthouse tower as well as any outbuildings such as the keeper's quarters, fog-signal building, fuel storage building and boathouse.

Nautical Mile: A unit of distance which is the average distance on the Earth's surface represented by one minute of latitude. It is equal to 1.1508 statute miles and mainly used at sea.

Nominal Range: The distance a light can be seen in good weather.

Occulting Light: A light in which the period of light is longer than the period of darkness and in which the intervals of darkness are all equal. Also known as an eclipsing light.

Order: A description of the power of the Fresnel lens ranging from one to seven from stronger to weaker.

Parabolic Reflector: A metal bowl shaped to a parabolic curve which reflects a lamp's light from it's center.

Parapet: A railed walkway which surrounds the lamp room.

Period: The total time for one cycle of the pattern of the light or sound signal.

Pharologist: A person with an interest in lighthouses.

Range Lights: Two lights which form a range provide direction to mariners for safe passage. They are described as the Front and Rear Lighthouses or the Inner and Outer. The front range light is lower than the rear, and when they align,the ship is in the proper position.

Revetment: A bank of stone laid to protect a structure against erosion from waves.

Revolving Light: A flash produced by the rotation of a Fresnel lens.

Riprap: Broken rocks or stone placed to help prevent erosion.

Sector: The portion of the sea lit by a sector light.

Skeleton Tower: Towers consisting of four or more braced feet with a beacon on top. They have little resistance to the wind and waves, and bear up well in a storm.

Solar-powered Optic: Many automated lights are run on solar powered batteries.

Spider Lamp: A brass container holding oil and solid wicks.

Tender: A ship which services lighthouses.

Ventilator: Opening' at the top of a lighthouse tower to provide heat exhaust and air flow within the tower.

Wick Solid: A solid cord which draws fuel to the flame in spider lamps.

Image Credits:

Alessio Damato: A coruna torre de hercules
Canadian Coast Guard: Sisters Islets
Keely Hill: Race Rocks
KenWalker: Chrome Island
Len@Loblolly Photo: Scarlett Point
Letterofmarque: Sambro Island
Louise Janes: Entrance Island
Paper ripper: Cape Beale
Smably: Sheringham Point
Thiersch; Pharos
Tim Gage: Estevan

All other images by the author

The Photographer's and Explorer's Series

Unless noted, there are Print and eBook editions available for the following.

Birds
Birding Guide to Orkney
Guide to Photographing Birds

Covered Bridges
Alabama Covered Bridges (eBook only)
California Covered Bridges (eBook only)
Canada's Covered Bridges
Connecticut Covered Bridges (eBook only)
Georgia Covered Bridges (eBook only)
Illinois Covered Bridges (eBook only)
Indiana Covered Bridges
Iowa Covered Bridges (eBook only)
Maine Covered Bridges (eBook only)
Massachusetts Covered Bridges (eBook only)
Michigan Covered Bridges (eBook only)
Minnesota Covered Bridge (eBook only)
New Brunswick Covered Bridges
New England Covered Bridges
Covered Bridges of the Mid-Atlantic
Quebec Covered Bridges
Covered Bridges of the South
Missouri Covered Bridges (eBook only)
New Hampshire Covered Bridges
New York Covered Bridges
Ohio's Covered Bridges
Oregon Covered Bridges
The Covered Bridges of Kentucky (eBook only)
The Covered Bridges of Kentucky and Tennessee
The Covered Bridges of Tennessee (eBook only)
Vermont's Covered Bridges
The Covered Bridges of Virginia (eBook only)
The Covered Bridges of Virginia and West Virginia
Washington Covered Bridges (eBook only)
The Covered Bridges of West Virginia (eBook only)
West Coast Covered Bridges
Wisconsin Covered Bridges (eBook only)

Lighthouses

Lighthouses of British Columbia
Maine Lighthouses
New Brunswick Lighthouses
Newfoundland Lighthouses
Nova Scotia Lighthouses
Ontario Lighthouses
Orkney and Shetland Lighthouses (eBook only)
Prince Edward Island Lighthouses
Scotland Lighthouses

Old Mills

Ontario's Old Mills

Ontario Waterfalls

Ontario Waterfalls

Index

www.ingramcontent.com/pod-product-compliance
Lightning Source LLC
La Vergne TN
LVHW081349060426
835508LV00017B/1490

* 9 7 8 1 9 2 7 8 3 5 5 9 3 *